Edwin D. Phillips

Texas and Its Late Military Occupation and Evacuation

Edwin D. Phillips

Texas and Its Late Military Occupation and Evacuation

ISBN/EAN: 9783337426583

Printed in Europe, USA, Canada, Australia, Japan

Cover: Foto ©ninafisch / pixelio.de

More available books at **www.hansebooks.com**

TEXAS,

AND ITS

LATE MILITARY OCCUPATION

AND

EVACUATION.

BY AN OFFICER OF THE ARMY.

NEW YORK:
D. VAN NOSTRAND, 192 BROADWAY.
1862.

TEXAS,

AND ITS

LATE MILITARY OCCUPATION

AND

EVACUATION.

BY AN OFFICER OF THE ARMY.

NEW YORK:

D. VAN NOSTRAND, 192 BROADWAY.

1862.

These pages have been hurriedly written from memory; and contain, I have no doubt, many errors. I designed in writing them, an explanation of the circumstances which attended the surrender of the regulars, and found that in this connection some general description of the country was necessary.

West Point, *July*, 1862.

Edwin D. Phillips,
Captain 1st *Infantry U. S. A.*

TEXAS,

In 1790 the Jesuit Missions, successively established northward of the Rio Grande during many
preceding years, extended to the head-waters of the
Nuéces and the San Saba, and reached nearly to the
Sabine river and the sea. The happy influence
which the Fathers had acquired over the Indians,
seems to have been used with such complete and
unremitting devotion to their welfare, that over
their native prairies, they had learned to tend large
herds and flocks; while they looked with wonder
upon unwonted scenes of wild peace and quiet, of
the real nature and cause of which, they could have
had no just appreciation.

They still make upon their powder-horns the or- ·

nament of the Cross; and have within recent years,
painted upon the high cliffs of the Concho, the rude
picture of a Mission House with its bell and rope—
over the roofless ruins of which the rank cactus has
climbed for years.

This happy and peaceful period had nearly ex-
pired when the insurrection of the Spanish colonies
began—for the gradual withdrawal, for the protection of the Capital of Mexico, of the few Spanish
troops who had been quartered at the Missions sub-
jected the faithful priests first to insult, and finally
to savage cruelty, until all had been murdered,
driven across the inhospitable wastes to the westward, or compelled to seek a refuge in the sand isl-
ands along the southern coast; and the country re-
lapsed into a wilderness, inhabited by wild beasts,
and Indians scarcely less so, in their unrestrained
freedom. Its vast area is more than three times great-
er than that of the six New England States, embrac-
ing besides its large tracts devoted to the culture of
corn, wheat, cotton, and sugar, nearly one hundred
and seventy-five millions of acres of uncultivated land.
No small portion of its territory was titled by the
authorities of Spain and Mexico, or granted in orig-

inal acts of its own Congress and Legislature; and
still the public domain numbers perhaps not much
less than one hundred millions of acres. Its surface
is a vast slope; the western limits of which, in the
barren regions of the Llano Estacado, are four thousand five hundred feet, and its central portions two
thousand feet above the sea. The coast range along
the Gulf of Mexico is a level prairie, extending fifty
miles into the interior, intersected by the large
rivers, but nearly destitute of timber, if we except
the small evergreen mesquite tree—a species of the
acacia—which, encumbered in all its branches with
the mistletoe, springs in every conceivable locality.
Many cool springs and beautiful fresh and salt water
lakes are met with in this prairie; and many wild
flowers, which in their wealth of fragrance compen-
sate the lack of names, bloom in profusion during
nearly the whole year. The region of high rolling
plains, of detached hills, and of groves of the dwarf
live-oak succeed, and within three hundred miles,
mountains of moderate height, rocks, and small rapid
streams abound, valleys and aroyas intervene, and
the most charming landscapes everywhere appear.
Still farther on, the country becomes more broken

and difficult of access, until through six hundred
miles of peculiar and diversified scenery, we ap-
proach the most inhospitable regions in the Staked
Plains of Texas and New Mexico. The state pos-
sesses perhaps very little of commercial interest;
has but few ports worthy of notice, among which
may be mentioned those of Galveston, Indianola, La-
vaca, Brownsville, and the villages of Matagorda
Bay, and the connection of these with the interior
is of the most indifferent and inadequate description.
The villages, and indeed most of the settlements, are
in the east; the wilderness is in the middle and
the west; and under heaven there can be no land
which merits more the name—more wild, and beautiful, and unavailable.

Extending from the latitude of 25° 45′ through
nearly eleven degrees to the northward, and having
so great an elevation, the softness and purity of its
varied climate may seldom be equalled, and can
scarcely be surpassed. The periodical northers oc-
cur between the months of September and March,
formed by the descent of cool air, which upon reaching the plains, hurries forward to the current of the
trade-winds; and during the warmer months, moist

breezes from the ocean supply the place of the heat-
ed air ascending from the prairie, and of the much
needed summer rains, until farther to the westward
they have, in climbing the Cordilleras ranges, lost
all their moisture. These changing winds prevail
as far westward as the north-eastern portion of the
Staked Plains, to the mouth of the Pecos, and along
the Sierra Madre to the sea. Mr. Thorpe, in his ac-
count of the Broca Chica and the Brazos Santiago,
remarks as to these restless winds along the coast,
that "there seems ever to be some troubled spirit in
the waters and air, that throws about the voyager's
craft, and makes him cautious in his movements."
It is indeed the most difficult and hazardous coast
with which I am acquainted. Such are some of the
general characteristics of Texas; deficient in large
navigable rivers, in safe and capacious harbors, in
railroads, in timber, in regular supplies of rain, in
nearly every thing which may make available the
resources of a country, however poor and barren :
abounding in every thing which nature may supply
for the wonder of her peculiar votaries.

In July, 1845, Texas, by the action of its own
Congress ratifying the joint resolutions of the Con-

gress of the United States, entered the Union, and
became entitled to claim from it that military protection which its own government had been power-
less to render during the period of its existence as a
separate republic. The Indians, occupying four-
fifths of its territory, had hitherto prescribed the ut-
most limit of the settlements, but now the throng
of domestic and foreign emigration pressing forward
to imaginary sources of wealth in the valleys of its
upper streams—the commercial advantages presented in its roads to North Mexico and Santa Fé, and,
over all, the adventurous restlessness by which its
unfixed population has ever been actuated—induced
those earnest appeals with which she sought the aid
of the general government, and in compliance with
which, between the date of the conclusion of the
peace with Mexico and the close of the year 1860,
there had been stationed in her territory, five regiments of infantry, two regiments of dragoons, the
regiment of mounted riflemen, and two regiments
of artillery. With the exception of the extreme
upper positions, the points occupied by the troops
were upon four consecutive lines of about seventy-
five miles, one hundred and fifty miles, two hundred

and seventy-five miles, and four hundred miles from the coast, and nearly parallel to its general direction. The very numerous positions which these lines embraced were not taken in consequence of the opinions of the department commanders; but the troops were perhaps pushed out very far beyond the natural limits of just military occupation, by the clamors of the restless people ; and the policy of distributing the troops in weak lines, which, traced upon a map, would embrace more than three thousand miles, being once adopted, might not be carelessly relinquished, since every real or projected settlement in the vicinity of the posts must otherwise be abandoned or frustrated. Meantime, the communication of the scattered garrisons with the headquarters of the department and with the states, was by the means of express mules and by the way of the prairie.

The political relations of Texas with the general government, had been distinguished by a reliant faith in the efficiency and the justness of the Federal laws, and a pride in her connection with the family of the states, which rendered her poorest people exultant in time of peace, and would have placed them foremost in deeds of daring in the event of foreign war.

In the beginning of the year 1861, she had at the head of her state government, a gentleman of unquestioned abilities, of much experience, and of profound discretion. Whatever may have been the political aspirations of General Houston, and however perplexing the paths in which he is said to have sought their attainment, his fearless and continued advocacy of the union of the states will be remembered in the land where he is buried, when the distinguishing policies pursued by many who surrounded him shall have ceased to avail their reputation, or to evoke their memory.

Nor are the subsequent acts of Lieutenant-Governor Clarke, who succeeded him, to be construed as more or less than the acknowledgment of the decrees of the improperly constituted assemblages in whose hands he had been placed. Around him were convened a legislature, made up for the most part of disappointed politicians from abroad; and a convention, whose members represented, with few exceptions, the wishes of no classes of the community—whose homes supplied them no other patrimony than the privilege of ruining, within its legislative halls, their native state; they were, how-

ever, the educated men who swayed the ignorant
masses of the people; their measures were taken
with the extremest circumspection, and prosecuted
with such vigor, that within a few days, almost the
entire population may be said to have been under
arms.

The convention appointed three commissioners,
who were instructed to demand the surrender of all
the public property within the limits of the state.
The commissioners found it extremely difficult to
force the commanding general to any definite action;
for with his habitual caution, he avoided committing
himself upon paper, and when pressed to act, he
usually said, "I will give up every thing," and the
exertions of Colonel Nichols, Assistant Adjutant-
General, in all probability prevented a much more
disgraceful capitulation than that which followed.
In justice to General Twiggs, it may be remarked,
that he constantly stated that, in the perplexing
emergencies of his situation, he had repeatedly dispatched his staff-officers to the seat of the general
government, with instructions to unfold the various
difficulties under which he labored; and requesting
specific instructions as to the future conduct of af-

fairs, which, with every succeeding day, were becoming more complicated.

On the 18th of February, General Twiggs, from his headquarters in San Antonio, issued a general order, to the effect that the state of Texas, having through its commissioners demanded the delivery of the military posts and the public property within its limits; and the commanding general being desirous of avoiding even the possibility of a collision between the Federal and the state troops, the posts would be evacuated by their garrisons, and the latter would take up, as soon as the necessary preparations could be made, the line of march out of Texas by way of the coast (marching out with their arms, the light batteries with their guns), clothing, camp and garrison equipage, quarter-master's, subsistence, medical, and hospital stores, and such means of transportation of every kind as might be necessary for an efficient and orderly movement of the troops, prepared for attack or defence against aggressions from any source, and carrying with them provisions as far as the coast. Simultaneous with this order, appeared a circular of the commissioners, stating that, having been fully empowered by the state of Texas to ex-

ercise the authority which they had undertaken,
they had formally and solemnly agreed with brevet
Major-General David E. Twiggs, U. S. Army, commanding the department of Texas, that the troops
of the United States should leave the soil of the
state by way of the coast, that they should take
with them the arms of the respective corps, including the battery of light artillery at Fort Duncan, and
the battery of the same description at Fort Brown ;
and should be allowed the necessary means for regular and comfortable movement—provisions, tents,
etc., etc., and transportation. The public property
at the various posts, other than that above mentioned, to be turned over to agents, to be appointed by
the commission; and who would render due and
proper receipts to the officers of the army, whom
they would relieve from the custody of the public
property. This order and circular did not reach the
military posts until several weeks after their pro-
mulgation.

Meantime a general order, dated at the War Department, January 28th, relieving General Twiggs
from the command of the department of Texas, and
directing Colonel Carlos A. Waite, of the first regi-

ment of infantry, to assume the command, reached the headquarters in San Antonio; and so soon as the commissioners became aware of the nature of this . order, measures were taken to intercept the express-man bearing the order to Colonel Waite, whose regimental headquarters were on the Verde Creek, a tributary of the Guadalupe River, and about sixty-five miles from San Antonio. These measures were frustrated by the foresight of Colonel Nichols, who had taken the precaution to send two separate expresses; the first was captured and taken back to San Antonio, but the second one reached Camp Verde at twelve o'clock M., on the 17th of February, and within three hours thereafter, Colonel Waite, escorted by a detachment of cavalry, took the road to San Antonio, where he arrived between one and two o'clock P. M., on the 18th, and found that all negotiations were closed, and that General Twiggs had surrendered all of the posts and the public property to the state of Texas; that the town was occupied by a large force of Texan troops, and that strong guards had been placed over the ordnance and ordnance stores, the clothing depot, and the commissary and quartermaster's departments, including means of transportation of every kind; while the two companies of United States regulars had been withdrawn from the town, and were encamped at some distance from the public stores. General Twiggs' order, relinquishing the command and transferring it to Colonel Waite, was issued on the 19th of February, and on the same-day the latter assumed command of the department, and from this time all the efforts of this faithful and accomplished officer were directed to the safe removal of the troops from Texas.

In the latter part of 1859, all the means of transportation (mules and wagons) at the military posts, over and above such as were indispensable for the purposes of hauling fuel and water for the use of the troops, and for the carrying of the mails, had, in compliance with a circular issued from the quartermaster's office at the department headquarters, been transferred to the general depot in San Antonio; so that the spring of 1861 found the scattered garrisons destitute of the means necessary for protracted marches across western and middle Texas, but ample provisions for this emergency were found in the stipulations which had been arranged be-

2

tween General Twiggs and the commissioners. In
the circular of the latter, and in the general order of
the late commander of the department for the evacuation of the posts, and Colonel Waite having speedily
arranged his plans for the movement of the troops,
lost no time in urging upon the commissioners a
prompt compliance with the agreement into which
they had entered, and the immediate dispatch of the
necessary means of transportation, which were now
completely under their own control.

It is not known that the commissioners deliber-
ately planned to delay the transportation, which
had to be sent in some instances to distances of
more than six hundred miles; but it is certain that
the trains were gotten in readiness and dispatched
up the country with such slowness as to warrant
the conclusion that they were at the least by no
means desirous for the speedy departure of the
troops. Some extenuation of the course which they
pursued in this, as well as in many subsequent trans-
actions, all tending to embarrass the action of the
department commander, may be had in the anxiety
which they may have felt for the safety of the settlements, which, with the sudden withdrawal of the

troops, must be exposed to the incursions of the
Indians; still, it is perhaps natural to presume, that
they conceived all delays to be favorable to the
purpose, which they doubtless entertained, of per-
suading a portion of the troops to join their cause.
"They are," say the commissioners in their circular
letter of the 18th of February, "our friends, who
have hitherto afforded us all the protection in their
power; and it is our duty to see that no insult or
indignity is offered them."

Early in April, Earle Van Dorn, late major in the
regular service, an officer of much distinction in the
Indian campaigns, who had thrown up his commission on the secession of his native state of Missis-
sippi, reappeared upon the coast of Texas, and
openly avowed his intention to take with him such
companies of the regulars as his abundant reputation might enable him to entice into the service of
the Confederate States, and, as if by preconcerted
arrangement, the San Antonio newspapers immediately teemed with articles designed to explain, that
in the great emergencies which were ensuing, the
soldiers were naturally relieved from the oaths of
allegiance which they had taken, and were at perfect

liberty to quit the service of the United States.
About this time, Lieutenant Thornton A. Washington, quartermaster of the first regiment of infantry,
who, in the implicit confidence of his commanding
officer, had been detached as quartermaster to the
port of Indianola, and who was fully depended upon
for the transaction of all business relative to the
embarkation of the troops, sent in his resignation,
and quitted his post and the public property con-
signed to his care. But it is not proposed in this
connection to enumerate the various difficulties
which surrounded the troops, and embarrassed their
able commander. How many of these difficulties
and impediments may have resulted from the preconcerted action of individuals, previous to the secession of the state, I am not able to say. Major Barnard,
in his interesting "Letter to an English Friend," remarks: "Mr. Floyd had taken care that the army
should not be available to his successor. It was scattered on our distant frontiers, and the capture of a
large portion in Texas was managed through the
agency of its commanding officer, a worthy accom-
plice and compeer in infamy of such a chief." Meantime the troops, on receiving their transportation,

marched rapidly down the country, by the way of
the El Paso road, by Fort Mason and Fredericks-
burgh, and by Eagle Pass and Brownsville. The
light batteries, the cavalry, and a portion of the infantry, reached the coast in time to embark on the
first steamers which arrived, and sailed for the
North with sealed orders, while the remainder of the
troops, consisting of two companies of the .first,
three companies of the third, and nine companies of
the eighth regiments of infantry, were still on the
march for the camp of rendezvous at Green Lake,
about thirty miles from the coast.

Among the earliest dispositions made by Colonel
Waite, on assuming the command of the department, had been the selection of this position at Green
Lake, and its occupation by the two companies of
infantry recently composing the garrison of San
Antonio barracks, commanded by brevet Major
Larkin Smith, of the eighth, a gentleman whose
high qualities have for years been the theme of his
own corps, but whose subsequent action I am not
able to explain; for immediately after breaking up
his camp, near the middle of April, and while under orders from his immediate commander at the

coast, to proceed to Washington, with verbal dis-
patches to the government, he suddenly threw up
his commission, and soon afterward entered the service of the Confederate States.

Near the middle of April the last of the troops
destined to constitute the next shipment reached
the vicinity of Indianola, and Major Sibley of the
third, senior officer, immediately sent forward the
baggage; and the troops, consisting of two companies of the first, and the adjutant and non-commissioned staff and band of the same regiment,
three companies of the third, and two companies
of the eighth, marched through the town, and
sleeping at night upon the long wharf, early in
the next morning went on board of the two small
steam lighters which had been chartered for their
use, and proceeded down Matagorda Bay, to embark on the steamer "Star of the West," which,
guarded by the Gunboat Mohawk, had for two weeks
been lying off the bar awaiting their arrival. But on
reaching the mouth of the harbor, twenty-five miles
below Indianola, they saw no sign of either of these
steamers, a circumstance which, though it created
some uneasiness in the minds of the officers, and was

somewhat dispiriting to the men, was in itself insuffi-
cient to justify any reasonable apprehension of bad
faith on the part of the people; for it was known that
in the constantly prevailing coast winds, the Star of
the West had, since her arrival off the bar, twice
parted her cables and gone to sea; and the Mohawk, obliged to keep up steam constantly, had in
all probability exhausted her supply of fuel, and
gone to Havana for coal. More reasonable grounds
for suspicion might have been entertained in connection with the behavior of the harbor pilots, had
these been characterized by as much of vigilance
and intelligence as distinguish the pilots in northern waters, for many of them were absent from
their stations, and the information afforded by
those who remained was exceedingly unsatisfactory;
facts, however, which as relating to Texan pilots
were not very surprising. However, Major Sibley
at once decided to go to sea in the lighters, and
make for the port of Tampico, on the coast of Mexico,
two or three hundred miles below the mouth of the
Rio Grande, at which port was a United States
consul, and where it was presumed vessels might
be obtained to convey the troops to the North.

There were at this time crowded upon these two small lighters seven companies of infantry, with their arms and camp equipage, the non-commissioned staff and band of one regiment, and not less than thirty laundresses. Only one day's supply of provisions and water for the troops had been taken, as the Star of the West had on board for their use some twenty thousand rations; and as the terms of the late capitulation did not permit the taking of any supplies whatever beyond the coast. Soon after Major Sibley had taken the resolution to proceed to Tampico, he ascertained that neither of the lighters had more than five or six hours' coal on board, and there remained to him no other course than to abandon his project, and returning to Indianola to take possession of his supplies while he had the power of reaching them; for the low, sandy, and almost impassable shores of Matagorda Bay afford no means of sustenance, and even the water is very impure and brackish. Accordingly the lighters returned, and in the same evening the troops disembarked, and taking possession of their supplies, encamped near Indianola; and the next day Lieutenant Whipple of the third, with a

small guard, was dispatched down the bay to watch
for the appearance of the transport and the gunboat.
This officer soon returned with very important information. No sign of either steamer was visible;
but he had ascertained that two or three pieces of
cannon had been placed in position upon the wharf
at Saluria, so as to command the channel near its
entrance to the sea.

This demonstration of hostile intentions appeared
conclusive, and Major Sibley immediately detached
Lieutenant Whipple with as many men as a small
yacht could accommodate, with orders to take advantage of the favorable wind which was blowing,
and under cover of the night to land at Saluria and
capture the guns; and before daylight in the morning, Captain Bowman of the third, with forty men,
was sent forward to support him, should his assist-
ance be necessary. In the evening both expedi-
tions returned; Lieutenant Whipple having ascertained that the guns had been removed, probably
up St. Mary's bayou, or by a sloop to La Vaca.

Meantime Major Sibley had taken possession of
the only means of transportation in the harbor,
with which it was practicable to go to sea, con-

sisting of two schooners of about one hundred and
fifty tons burden each, recently from northern
ports, and only one of which had discharged her
cargo. A strong guard occupied the long wharf,
and a fatigue party of a hundred men was detached for the work of unloading the freighted
schooner, which continued all night, and so soon
as this work was accomplished, and the necessary
supplies were placed on board, the troops em-
barked, and, towed by the lighters, the two
schooners proceeded down the bay. Strong south-
easterly winds were blowing across the bar, and
the weather outside was evidently stormy; but
long before reaching the lower bay, the masters
of the schooners had informed Major Sibley, that
with their overcrowded decks, the schooners could
not possibly be managed in the open sea; but
that in case an additional transport could be pro-
cured to take off a portion of the troops, they
would have no hesitation in attempting to pass
the channel of the bar, even without pilots, and
though they were but slightly acquainted with the
coast. However, night came on before the vessels
had reached the vicinity of the bar, over which the

rapid surf was pushing, and the darkness soon
made it impossible for the lighters to tow them
through its narrow channel. They anchored at
dark, and Captain Bowman, of the third, and
Lieutenant Greene, of the first, with a detachment of thirty men, were sent on board one of
the lighters, and taking advantage of this necessary delay, were directed to proceed up the bay
and bring down a brig which was known to be
somewhere above, and might have reached Indianola since the departure of the schooners. The
next day presented no indications of more favorable weather; however, a steamer's smoke was
visible to the seaward, and it was presumed that
the Star of the West or the Mohawk was ap-
proaching the coast. As the day wore on, the
steamer closed under the projecting strips of land
to the south-eastward, though nothing but the
dense smoke from her stacks was visible; not a
solitary sail appeared in the offing, and no pilots
came near the vessels. Detachments of troops
were sent off in the boats of the schooners to fill
the water barrels which had been emptied, as
there was on board scarcely a sufficient supply

for Key West or Havana. Meantime the remaining lighter had nearly exhausted her fuel, and was let go; and during the afternoon the appearance of the other lighter, with the brig, was anxiously expected; but night at length closed in with no signs of either, while the wind across the narrow, crooked channel of the dangerous bar was still freshening. At ten o'clock, though the night was dark, dense volumes of smoke were seen not far above the schooners, and a boat, with a small party, commanded by Lieutenant Hopkins, of the third, left the commanding officer's schooner to ascertain the cause. This careful and sagacious officer soon returned with the information that several steamers were anchored above the schooners, and it was now apparent that Captain Bowman's detachment had been captured, and that the schooners were entrapped to the windward, by the steamer which had been supposed the Star of the West, and in the other direction by the steamers which had arrived in the night. At daylight three steamers were seen at anchor five hundred yards above the schooners, each having on a full head of steam, their

double decks surrounded with tiers of cotton-
bales, and bearing, as is believed, the pieces of
cannon which were mentioned as having been
at Saluria some days previous.

Later in the morning the large steamer which
had been lying outside passed the bar, and, with
steam up, anchored three hundred yards to the
windward of the schooners, bearing upon her decks
one twenty-four-pounder and two field-pieces. The
Texan troops on board of the four steamers numbered between one thousand and fourteen hundred
men, supplied with various kinds of fire-arms, and
having between three and seven pieces of cannon.
The regulars on the two schooners numbered not far
from three hundred men, armed with the rifle and
bayonet; still it is presumed the latter had been
something more than a match for their opponents
could they have met them in the field. The steamers
possessed, however, the capability of running around
the schooners, and of sinking either of them before
she could get under way; and there was therefore
nothing left but to accede to the formal demand
which had been made in the morning by Earle Van
Dorn, colonel in the Confederate States army, com-

manding the Texan troops in Matagorda Bay, through his commissioners, who came off to the schooners under a flag of truce. The terms of the capitulation were accordingly arranged in the course of the day, and Major Sibley, with the approval of all of his officers, surrendered; the Texans, besides capturing the troops, obtaining by this affair more than three hundred fine rifles, with equipments, and the camp equipage of seven companies of infantry.

The particulars of this first surrender have been thus minutely related, in consequence of the somewhat severe strictures which appeared in the newspapers, and which did not, so far as has been observed, attach to the other column of seven companies of the eighth, under Lieutenant Colonel Reeve, which was still (late in April) marching down the El Paso road. Indeed, the particulars of the capture of the last-named column can need no lengthy recital; for, on its reaching middle Texas, in the month of May, the supplies necessary to its advance were in the hands of the agents of the Confederate States; while, at the smallest estimate, fifteen thousand men, with two splendid batteries of light

artillery, opposed its march in any direction. To
have advanced into the settlements with his command of three or four hundred men, would have
been more prudent in Colonel Reeve, than without
supplies to have retreated toward the Rio Grande;
and either course would have been alike preposter-
ous, and he accordingly surrendered.

On the 23rd of April, one day previous
to the capture of the first column of the troops,
Colonel Waite, with his staff, and all of the officers on duty at San Antonio, were made prisoners,
under circumstances peculiarly aggravating; for,
to the declarations of the former, that neither himself nor his staff-officers could even perceive the
validity of the claim which their captors assumed
to the exercise of the delegated authority of the
Congress of Montgomery, it was only replied, that
it should, at the least, be made apparent that he
and the other gentlemen were prisoners; and that
physical force should not be wanting as a full and
sufficient argument, in the circumstances of the apparent distrust, which was exhibited in the agents
of the Confederate States; one of whom, Major
Maclin, had until quite recently retained his com-

mission as paymaster, in the service of the United States.

Of course, the discussions which ensued were unavailing; nor could appeal be had from these agents, to a people who perceived only their first men leading the way toward that object, which the latter blinded their own eyes in pursuing, and which the ignorant had been taught to imagine they beheld in the full light of justice and reason; for party heat, and the frenzy, which have been displayed upon less grave political questions in happier times, found here no wise examples of restraint, but every encouragement to their indulgence.

Colonel Waite, and the officers at San Antonio, as well as the officers and men of Major Sibley's command, were permitted, should they desire it, the privilege of returning to the North on parole; every inducement being at the same time presented for the troops to quit their allegiance and enter the service of the Confederate States.

The giving and the receiving of a parole must be matter of equal delicacy; for he who from a sense of duty, or who, actuated by interested motives, may ask a pledge of honor from another, must be

sensible of a power which he is wielding, which
makes up for the disinclination to acquiescence in
the other; and he who shall render such a pledge
must be aware that he will purchase at the price of
an equal power, all of the privileges and the immu-
nities which it may be equal to; and it is presumed
that no one would consent to give his parole, who
should be aware that in refusing to do so, he might
subserve any interest of his government: but if in
giving it he yield no such interest, it is conjectured
there may often be no reasonable grounds for with-
holding it. Colonel Waite and the officers at San
Antonio, as well as the officers and men of Major
Sibley's command, were paroled. The latter officer
obtained an additional transport for his troops, and
so soon as the necessary arrangements could be
made, the vessels passed the bar and proceeded to
sea: they reached New York harbor in a voyage of
thirty days. Colonel Reeve's command, which was
captured in May, comprised all of the remaining
troops who occupied the department of Texas.
They were not permitted to return on parole, but
were held as close prisoners at San Antonio. The
Texans had now captured fourteen companies of the

regulars, including two companies of the first, three companies of the third, and nine companies of the eighth regiments of infantry, numbering, perhaps, not far from seven hundred men, with rifles, camp equipage, and ordnance stores; and the United States no longer held military possession of the state.

During the years of its occupation by the troops, the state had steadily advanced in prosperity, and all of its natural resources had been most rapidly developed, until from having been in 1845 almost without a foreign commerce, the value of her exports to Great Britain alone, in 1860, cannot have been far short of ten millions of dollars, while her trade with New Orleans and the various Northern ports may have amounted to five millions more.

Post-offices and judicial tribunals had been established in the new counties which were constructed as the troops advanced westward, and large tracts of land embraced within their limits, not suited to the production of the cereal grains, supplied in every season of the year abundant pasturage, to immense herds of beef cattle and horses.

The disorderly population of former years had become a law abiding people, who, emulous in all the advantages of cultivated life, had grown observant of the rules and customs which are prescribed for their attainment.

With the withdrawal of the troops from Texas, her days of progress were for the present numbered; the settlements were broken up, and twenty years of the returning peace, may scarcely suffice to replace them.